Spot the Difference

Raising your game to reach your full Potential

Swiss – So solid

Spot the Difference

Raising your game to reach your full Potential

Swiss – So solid

TamaRe House Publishers, 2008
Printed in the UK, 2008
info@tamarehouse.com
www.tamarehouse.com

Cover by Third I Design
mail@third-i-design.com

First Edition

ISBN 978-1-906169-43-5

Contents

9
Potential

Nine is the highest number to us, in the universe. There is no single digit higher than nine (9) because when we go beyond nine we actually start to use the digits below 9 to represent larger numbers. This is known as the binary system, the decimal system or base 10.

When counting up from zero (0) to nine (9), one (1) would be the first number as zero (0) is below one (1). So putting the two numbers together, gives the illusion that they are higher than 9 when they are not. Nine is the greater and higher number.

So there is no number greater or higher than the number 9. This is a fact! Nine is regarded a mystical number amongst many ancient cultures, one being the Egyptians, it represents completion. For example, it takes nine months for a baby's full growth in the womb of its mother. Nine is a number when multiplied reproduces the same figure from up to down and from down to up, and equals itself.

$$9 \times 5 = \underline{45} \qquad 9 \times 6 = \underline{54}$$
$$9 \times 4 = 36 \qquad 9 \times 7 = 63$$
$$9 \times 3 = 27 \qquad 9 \times 8 = 72$$
$$9 \times 2 = 18 \qquad 9 \times 9 = 81$$
$$9 \times 1 = 9 \qquad 9 \times 10 = 90$$

Nine is the only number that can do this. If we take the answer of 9 x 2 which is 18, we will see that $1 + 8 = 9$ etc.

9 Potential is about reaching and accessing our full capacity through study and application. We can achieve and become anything we want if we acknowledge that making time to study ourselves and our environment is the key to unlocking our 9 Potential. This eventually gives us full access to our brain and DNA, which will make us supreme beings once again. At the moment scientist say most of us only use 5 to 7 percent of our brain which renders us very limited in the things we can do. NOW is the time to take ourselves to the next level.

This is what 9 Potential is all about. The books we are putting out is about knowing ourselves and the world around us, and becoming that perfect being that we're destined to be.

9 Knowledge

produces

9 Wisdom

produces

9 Overstanding

produces

9 Mind

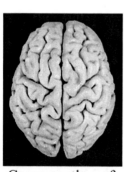

Cross-section of
the brain

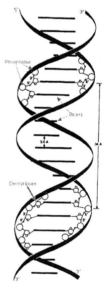

DNA double helix

Introduction

Whassup family! Greetings!

Thank you for opening this book. This book is a study book, so have a dictionary with you if possible and use it when you see words you do not understand. That is the only way we are going to learn and become familiar with the English Language.

Who is this book aimed at?
All youth, particularly Black youth.

Why is this book aimed at Black youth?
This book is aimed at Black youth of today although all cultures can learn something from it.

Throughout my growing up I have noticed that some of us, as young, Black people, are not seen to be achieving the same amount of 'success' as other groups in society. There is an apparent lack of unity amongst us. We all tend to fight down rather than help each other to get to where we need to be. It hasn't always been like this but in my lifetime I have seen this situation in the U.K, and across the world, get worse. It seems as though everyone speaks of the problem but the majority do not want to help come up with solutions. It seems as though there are no great black community leaders anymore, speaking out overtly about the real problems we face, or at least we don't really hear of them. Most are underground, doing great works within the U.K, but we don't recognise it. As a people, it looks as though we have given up trying to keep our race in the race of self-development, improvement and achieving.

We are poor, physically, mentally and spiritually. We have cut ourselves off from our greatness for some crazy reason and this has obviously translated down to the youth of today. Our lifestyle, actions and our minds are not as they should be. This is why we are acting the way we do currently. This book highlights some of the reasons why we are in the state we're in as young black people, at this present moment in time, and how to work our way out of it. This is so we can start to progress as individuals, families and as a race. If we take a look at ancient Africa it is easy to see that we are the pioneers of the modern world; we had the first schools, universities, hospitals and holy places, which mean's we had the first teachers, scientists, astronomers, doctors, priests, scribes and so on.

If we look at Africa and Black people across the world right now, it seems as if we are not the same, great people that we used to be. This is because we are not doing the great things that we did anymore, and the question we need to ask ourselves is: what on and above earth has happened?

How did we go from being and doing great things, to being and doing hardly anything considered of worth?

Something appears to have gone wrong along the way. We have neglected **our-story,** culture, mindset and way of life and replaced it with **his-story** mindset**,** culture and way of life.

When a people's account of greatness gets taken away from them, they have nothing great to look back on. This makes them feel they have no worth in the world. This is one of the reasons why we are the way we are at the moment. It seems as though our value in the world has disappeared. In school we learn nothing of ourselves as existing in times before slavery, if we are even taught properly about slavery itself. So when we look back at his-story in our Black minds, that's what we go back to; slavery, struggle, fight, oppression, fear, hatred etc.

It's like we are walking up a steep hill with all these psychological experiences weighing us down emotionally, spiritually and mentally. This book is about trying to support us in restoring that greatness by making clear simple principles that we can apply in working on our inner selves. If we can't handle the basics, then the complicated things cannot be addressed properly. The book is aimed at our youth because they are our future.

In this book we use the word **overstand** because we want you to get familiar with the word and act of **overstanding.** We feel that to **understand** something is to **stand under or beneath it,** when you literally dissect the word. To **stand under** or to be a student of what ever we are exposed to is not, we feel, to get the true meaning, reason and essence of what the words and lessons we are learning about. Therefore, we are forever looking up at things instead of getting a full view of what we are looking at, hence the use of the term **overstand**.

I don't know about you, but I don't want to be **standing under** any one I want to either stand level with you or **overstand** why, when, where, how and what you are doing and the reason behind it.
You get me?

I'm not saying **understanding** is a bad thing because when we are children we need to be taught how to understand persons, places and things, words and the world around us, however, once we have fully understood what we have learned and reached a certain age, we need to start learning about how to overstand persons places things, words and the world around us, which comes with knowledge and wisdom.

So to **overstand** is this, I'll tell you how it was taught to me.

What is the colour of the wall in your bedroom?

Your answer would probably be **blue, yellow, green, red** or something like that, yes?

Then I would say **NO!**

That's the colour of the paint. What's the colour of the wall?

Now that may sound confusing, but think about it.

Now you'd either say that you don't know or you might say something like '**white**'

Again, I would say **NO! That's the colour of the paint under the paint.**

What's the colour of the wall?

You would have to say, "**I don't know**"!

Now, to find out, we would have to scratch past the surface of what you can see right! That's what **overstanding** is about, scratching past the surface or illusion of what is in front of us. This means to know the mechanics behind the very thing we are studying and then probing further to see what else can be revealed to us. For example, right now you are reading a book with a whole load of words in it that make up the language we call English. As well as knowing these words it is useful to **overstand** the **etymology** of the words being read. This means knowing where the words come from; their roots in the language of origin. This is because the English language, has evolved from the French, Greek, Latin, German tongues that it has mixed with that all fall under the term Indo-European. There are also African words within it.

With our wall, remember **once we get past the paint, we will realise that there is plaster; plaster is made of lime and sand. Under the plaster is brick, the brick is made out of sand and clay.**

Well what's clay made of?
Various elements

What are elements?

The components that make up this physical world; you know, hydrogen, helium, carbon, oxygen...

Ok, smarty pants, what are elements made of?
Atoms

And what are atoms made of?
Protons, neutrons and electrons.

And what are protons, neutrons and electrons?
They are sub-atomic particles.

Well what does sub-atomic mean?
It means things that are below the mass (size) of an atom.

Do you **overstand**? We want to know how our world ticks; we shouldn't want to stop at the surface anymore. That would be to understand, **stand under**, that's ignorance. Remember we want to **overstand.** That's what **overstanding** is, as opposed to **understanding.**

When you start to **overstand** things, the way you look at the world changes, it widens our reality.

The kind of enquirer who wishes to go beyond the surface to the hidden meaning of things is the kind of person who is more likely to go on to be an initiator.

It is better to become the one that initiates change rather than the one that is affected by change without having a clue why, you get me?

So let's try and get the word **overstand** in the dictionary NOW. Let's be proactive and change things. It's a word that the Black community have been using for a long time, so it is nothing new.

Another word you will see within this book is the word **ourstory**. This is because we **overstand** that we as Black people have relied on our slave masters and their descendants to tell us the story of our past. We can't rely on them to tell us the when, why, what, how and where we came from! I'm not saying we can't hear their side of the story. I'm saying that's all we would be getting; **their** side, and we know that all stories have at least three sides:

1) Our side
2) Their side
3) The objective reality

So we want to know our side of the story so we can **overstand** what was the reality of what happened, **from our perspective**, hence the word **ourstory**.

I will ask you to humbly take your time in reading this book. Study it thoroughly so you can get the fullness of what we are trying to give to you, so you can overstand our story and be one of the change agents in the society in which you live. Let's enjoy our read.

Acknowledgments

Baba (Neter A'aferti Atum-re), my Mum, Amna, Auntie Pat, Shu, Charmain murry, Khonsu, Paul Simons, Donna Alexander, Mega, Gaien, Morgan, Danny, Femi, Rhea, 279, Cleopatra, Monde, Montu, Haru, Fuji, the students of Richmond college, Natalie, Shabz, Khnum and Geb.

Mindset

Chapter One

Before we start this chapter I think there is a question that we really need to ask ourselves.

AM I SCARED OF CHANGE?

First things first. In order to change, we have to want to change. No one can be forced to change; it's our personal choice. In taking a look at the world we live in it can be seen that changes are always happening. There are many changes in fashion: the way we dress our trainers, hair styles and in the cars we drive. We change our ring tones and we all know that the weather changes every so often. Change is constant. What would life be like if things didn't change?

VERY UNNATURAL!
So see change as a very healthy and positive thing.

"THE WORLD DOES NOT NEED TO CHANGE, YOU DO"

Most people are actually scared of change because they are attached to the self that they have gotten used to and project to others and by changing, they think they are going to lose their identity. Even if that change is a positive step towards making us better people, we are still scared to make it happen. This is because we usually live by the standards which we think other people would like us to live by, rather than what we know we should be aspiring to. Living like this actually makes us *reactive* people and not *proactive*. To be successful in anything we do, we need to be proactive.

The weather can stop us doing what we have planned to do, if we allow it to. How many times have we woken up, looked outside and been disheartened by the gloomy weather? Letting this affect how we carry out the rest of our day actually *makes* you gloomy too, right?

This too is reactive. Just because the weather is not so good doesn't mean our day should be bad. We should get used to Saying affirmations to ourselves like "I will not let the weather control my day!" this is a positive affirmation that, if said enough times, will fuel the motivational energy for us to complete the many tasks that we may have with in our day, regardless if the weather is good or not. If you don't like the affirmation I have given, make up some that means something to you, make sure it is positive and say it out loud to yourself. Be positive and proactive not negative and reactive don't let anything stop you from getting done what needs to be done.

When we talk about change, we are not saying that we are totally changing who and what we are. What we want to do is, be who we truly are, making sure we are using the experiences we go through to 'upgrade' and advance ourselves. We do not have to repeat the same pattern over and over again, making the same old mistakes and learning nothing from them.

Repeating bad habits causes us to become set in 'bad' ways and then we become the person who people say he/she doesn't know where they're are going in life.

DO YOU WANT TO BECOME THAT PERSON?

Remember change is good!
When we start becoming more proactive and embracing our change of habits the first people that are going to notice are our friends. Be aware of the type of friend that is around because the first thing a friend might ask is: **"Why are you acting different?"** Our answer to that can be: **"I have to act different, because if I stay the same I'm not going anywhere!"**

Or they might say: **"Who do you think you are now?"** And our answer can be: **"I'm the same person. I'm just trying to better myself."**

They might even say: **"What, do you think you are better than me now?"** Our answer can be, **"No, I'm not trying to be better than you, I'm trying to be better than I was before. I want to be the best me I can be!"**

Sometimes the best thing would be to stay away from the kind of person who will not encourage us through our transformation. The effect of such a person is to drain our confidence, bringing us back down to their level.

Look at it like this: when a caterpillar goes through its changes to become a butterfly it cuts itself off from the world by building for itself a cocoon. This is the same principle we can use. It is helpful to protect ourselves from anything that's going to stop us from improving and having a successful transformation; even if that means staying away from friends for a period of time, like the caterpillar. We can work on our inner being, strengthening our weaknesses, and just like that beautiful butterfly, that comes out at the end of the caterpillar's transformation, so will you be more beautifully transformed, if we give ourselves the time and make the effort.

Remember our brain is powerful, we can practically do anything we put our effort and time into, and it's all down to choice. We can either help our brain to destroy ourselves, or help it to do great things. Just like fire, we can use it to cook food or we can burn a house down with it. For example, when waking up in the morning, it's important to know what mindset we waking up in. Is it a positive or negative mindset?

This is important, because our mindset determines the way we are going to handle the situations that are in front of us. There will be times in our life when one chance to tackle an important challenge is present. If we are not in the right state of mind, then we will fail to meet our challenge adequately.

There will also be times when we will not be able to prepare for things and we will have to suddenly adapt in a given situation at a particular time. If we make the effort of always having a positive attitude, we will always perform to the best of our ability and tap into our hidden potential. Always remember to prepare for the tasks that are put ahead of you.

Music is something that can also affect us mentally. If we wake up listening to music that we know is going to have a negative effect on our mindset, (especially if we know we are easily influenced) it is probably best to replace it by listening to positive music, or, totally avoid it. The same goes for watching the T.V, reading newspapers and holding discussions with people.

Even if our thoughts are negative replace them with positive thoughts. It only takes one distraction to remove focus. It is very easy to be misled, if we are not in control.

See it like this. We have will power, which is basically our ability to make a choice between what we want to do, whether it is positive or negative.

"I will do positive"
"I won't do positive"

"I will do negative"
"I won't do negative"

And the choices we make will either swing our days, weeks, months or lives towards being positive and agreeable or negative and disagreeable. The choice is entirely in our hands, and it works like a domino effect once we make the choice. If we start our day thinking negative, then it's likely that our negative thoughts will swing our whole day towards being negative if we are not entirely aware of it.

To provide an image so it can be seen more clearly, picture our will power as a 360° degree circle with a vertical line down the middle. See page 19.

On the right side of the circle we have our positive choices and on the left side we have our negative choices and whatever we choose will determine our present or near future.

Having negative words and images in our brains can change our entire outlook on life, and have us become totally pessimistic, if we are not careful.

The battle of the mind is one of the hardest to win. We have to be careful of what we tempt it with. We also have to be very watchful of when we are trying to change our mindset. The old ways of our previous mindset is always trying to subtly creep its way back in. What we want to do when this happens is not battle with it, but simply to guide our thoughts back on course towards our goal.

Some of us might not know it, but music, T.V, newspapers and people have a great effect on how we deal with, look at and handle other people and situations. If we don't analyze what goes into our brains we probably won't analyze what comes out of our mouths which an extension of the brain. Always observe and think before you speak as well as listen more than you talk, that's why we have two ears, two eyes and only one mouth.

"USE YOUR HEAD OR STOP CARRYING IT AROUND WITH YOU"

Some of us as a people are not creating our own mindset; we are letting the outside world create it for us. Not being in control of our own lives means someone else is controlling it. We are therefore acting like robots. Our thoughts, actions and the way we live is not based on how we used to live as Black/African/Nuwbun/Ptahite people. We have been cut off from our ancient ways, and slowly taken up someone else's way of thinking and living, that's why so many of us are in a state of confusion

What we need to start doing is to take control of our lives: how we think, speak and act. This begins with being fully in control and overstanding of self, creating a positive mindset and being responsible for our actions. "Yes, I admit I was wrong." "Yes, I am going to do better." "Yes, I am proud of who I am." This is what we need to start telling ourselves. This is because our thoughts and mindsets are the base of everything we do. Thus positive thoughts create positive action.

In case you didn't know, the mind is our most powerful gift and thought is the most powerful force in the universe. The mind created everything that is around you!

It is mind that has created houses, computers, internet, cars, space rockets etc. The more time you spend on controlling the mind, the better it will work for you. Objective concentration is probably the best method to use in learning how to control it.

Did you know many scientists say that the average person cannot concentrate on a single thought for longer than 6 to 9 seconds per minute? Our brains are always racing, jumping from one thought to the next, we need to learn how to slow down our thoughts and expand our attention by practising concentration exercises.

(You can find an exercise at the back of the book on objective concentration. This will help better concentration and to expand attention.)

Will Power

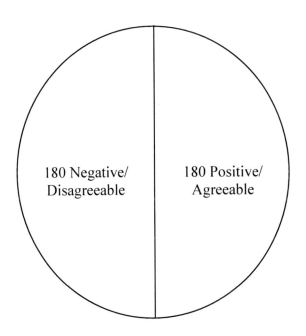

Will Power

Vocabulary

Chapter Two

Having a good vocabulary is one of the most important tools for use in progressing in today's society.

It separates the smart from the not so smart, the bright from the dim, and the intelligent from the un-intelligent.

Having a good vocabulary enables us to express our feelings in a clear manner. I feel, poor vocabulary is one of the reasons why so many of us are under achieving and so frustrated, because we are not able to articulate ourselves appropriately to communicate our thoughts to society.

When a person recognizes that we have a good vocabulary, they instinctively develop a level of respect for us and are more inspired to listen. This is a very important topic for me, being I have come from a street orientated background. I have noticed that some of us young Black men/women overly use street slang and hit a point in our lives where we fail to continue to learn the English language. Slang has actually become like a new language for us, which holds no real value in general society. This is one of the reasons, I feel, some of us are not progressing and this will eventually stop us from making a significant, and crucial, impact in the modern, business world. The use of slang is increasing on the street; it is like the spread of a virus infecting the vocabulary of young people. This forces us into using it to a greater extent to communicate with our friends. So it means we are going backwards rather than forwards. Basically we are heading nowhere fast. We are good at appearing un-intelligent, what we need to start doing is utilizing our potential to master the English language. A dictionary is one of the tools that we can use, to help stretch our vocabulary. I'm not saying don't use slang amongst ourselves. I'm saying know *when* to use it.

"MAKE LEARNING A FIRST IN YOUR LIFE"

To change this epidemic we need to start reading more. When we read more we become learners, as a learner, we become more open to taking in new things. In this way we can eventually become teachers. By becoming a teacher, we can re-teach ourselves some of the things that we already knew, but have now forgotten and pass our knowledge on to others. It is good practice to always have a dictionary, or even an encyclopaedia, at hand in the pursuit of knowledge.

The reason why we always have to pursue knowledge is because otherwise we keep on going round in circles and going back to what we already know or, even worse, stop learning. At this point a kind of decay sets in and the brain shrinks its capacity and starts dying. This is because it is not challenged and that is when we start limiting our potential. The brain likes a challenge. It likes to know when it successfully completes a challenge and likes taking on new challenges.

Keep it happy and alive by always keeping it active. We should hold conversations with elders for their wisdom and experience Instead of spending eighty per cent of our time listening to music, movies and people who do not stimulate our intelligence, read a book, widen your musical collection and visit a museum.

This is something I had to do myself, after finding that my capacity to engage in intelligent conversation was dropping rapidly. I wasn't giving any time to *my self* in studying anything but rapping, dee-jaying and producing music. I also smoked a lot of weed, which didn't do much for the parts of my brain that deals with memory, speech and other intelligence faculties.

I had to look at myself in the mirror and ask "what was I really doing to myself?" I had to ask myself "what example was I setting for my youngsters?" And "what kind of person would I be in the future?" I was a very smart, young man going through primary and secondary school. I was, however, far too easily influenced into doing stupid things. If you're anything like me please don't make the same mistakes.

Writing down your goals

Chapter Three

Before setting down this chapter, I'd like to highlight a dis-ease that we all suffer from as human beings. It is a dis-ease called fear.

Fear can be seen as a figment of our imagination that grows the more we pay attention to it. Fear is an attention seeker that needs attention because it wants to become a reality in order to make us believe it's real and that it can stop us from achieving and being confident within ourselves. Fear can also be seen as a test that our brain has created to see how we will deal with the possibility of not being able to reach our goal. It's actually testing our commitment, which in a way can be a good thing because if we can't overcome the obstacles in the brain, then it makes life's realities harder to deal with.

Ultimately fear is a thought and feeling about something we think is going to happen in the future and the truth is we don't know what is going to happen. We normally guess what we think is going to happen and when we get there it turns out to be nothing like that negative that we thought is was going to be.

So therefore it was a waste of time giving the thought our energy in the first place.

"DOUBT AND FEAR ARE GREAT ENEMIES"

Writing down our goals is one of the fundamental steps when striving to become the person we want to be. When we make the effort of doing this we are actually giving our mind a rest from going round in circles, we are confirming to ourselves what we want to do and that we are serious in the organising of doing it, thus stabilizing the first steps of our future.

This is something that many successful people do when starting any new venture or business they wish to pursue, it's a principle we should definitely incorporate in our life. Its similar to writing down a shopping list, except that our goals is not something that we can buy, we have to be very committed and work hard for them.

Writing down our goals is a reassurance to ourselves. We're also materialising our dream in words, strengthening that inner voice inside ourselves. When writing down our goals it's important to be realistic to ourselves also. It's not something we should be in any hurry to do; we need to really analyze where we are in the present moment of our lives and what is achievable to us. Think on it, and then write it down.

After writing down our goals look at the piece of paper and say each of the goals one at a time back to ourselves so we reaffirm our intention. In doing this we have actually made a full circle, let me tell you what I mean.

We produced our goals in our head. We materialised them on paper. And then we put them back inside our head, by saying them to ourselves, so now it is stamped for good. We can say it back to ourselves as much times as we please, the more we do it, the more impression it has on our sub-conscious mind.

What about the youngsters?

Chapter Four

What about the youngsters? What I would like for us as brothers and sisters to do, is stop this thinking and acting, as if the way we carry ourselves has no effect on the younger generations, it is very selfish and ignorant.
(I'm guilty of this myself)

As young Black males and females, I feel that we have a greater responsibility than any other race to make things better for Black people. As well as help our future (the children) climb the social ladder. Statistically our youth are not performing as good as other so called (ethnic minorities) in the U.K. They are going to prison rapidly and I think one of the main causes are: lack of good role models in many of our families as well as lack in adults understanding our young people and what they go through. Some of our parents don't put in enough work for their children. Mothers have to become the fathers in some cases, which make our women look strong as they are usually able to cope. However, single parent scenarios don't always show a good image for our youth. It can be very damaging, both mentally and physically for the mother and child, although some of us may not admit it.

The situation is no different with single parent fathers also. When a single parent is forced to play the mother/father role we are most likely going to see an imbalance in the child's life. In some cases our children may seek role models in peer groups/crews of street culture, which may lead to harmful situations and illegal activities.

If this sounds anything like your situation, whether your mother or father has not been able to be there for you, try not to use it as an excuse to do disagreeable things. We should look for other elders in our families or communities to help us gain wisdom and overstanding of how to deal with life.

You will be surprised how much helpful information we can get from our elders, that people our own age cannot give us, don't be scared to share what you are going through with someone that cares.

"HELP SAVE THE CHILDREN, IF FOR NO OTHER REASON THAN YOU WERE ONE"

Some T.V programmes, cartoons and games consoles can play major roles in our up bringing as well as those that are younger than us, which can be more damaging than progressive. So what kind of future are our progeny going to have, without a stable foundation?

You judge a tree by the fruit it bares and some of the fruit we are baring right now are stale.

This is the reason why some of our youth are taking up gang activity L.A style i.e., wearing colours to differentiate one from another drug trafficking, gun crime, robbery's etc. Are we that bored, uneducated or are we that dumb?

I've noticed on the street that youth gangs are taking up the names of American gangs, without knowing the meaning of these names or why these gangs were started. The B.L.O.O.D and C.R.I.P gang's are probably two of the largest black gangs in America that started as community organisations and have turned into rivals against each other. The B.L.O.O.D wear red and the C.R.I.P wear blue; if one is seen in another's territory then it's likely that the person will be assaulted. The B.L.O.O.D and C.R.I.P rivalry has resulted in hundreds of murders where black lives are taken unnecessarily. Sadly the same thing is happening with us in the U.K.

Both B.L.O.O.D and C.R.I.P are acronyms, which is a word formed from initial letters of other words. For example: B.L.O.O.D stands for "Brotherly Love Override Oppression and Destruction" And C.R.I.P stands for "Community Revolution in Progress."

As I said in the introduction, we need to start scratching past the surface of what is going on around us in order to overstand why, when, how and what is really happening on the surface, then we just might realise why these gangs are fighting against each other.

B.L.O.O.D and C.R.I.P gangs started as community organisations that protected the community from white oppressors. I would recommend you do some research on these gangs.

It seems we are a bunch of followers in the U.K with a very limited overstanding of the things we follow.

Come on family, we are better than this! Some of our parents or grandparent's have come to the UK and have done their best to get us where we are right now, so we need to start moving forward in the right direction, we need to protect, not destroy the legacy of our people.

Which brings me to my next point, legacy is something that gets handed down and I don't think some parents stress enough to us as young people what our role is, and how far they as parents and their parents have come in order to get us to the point we are right now. It would seem that some parents have become very complacent in the role of leaders in our communities and families.

Yes we have been tricked along the way many times as a race, but we are still here. This isn't about blaming our parents it's about recognising the mistakes and correcting them for future generations. Most of our parents and families have fed us clothed us given us wisdom, love, a roof over our heads and paid the rent. I think its time we start returning the "favour" (for lack of a better word).

Let us start respecting our selves, learning ourstory, so we can appreciate how and why we got here and work towards buying property and owning successful business's, so mummy and daddy can go home to Africa or the Caribbean and build homes and business's for themselves if its there choice or stay here and put up their feet. It's not going to happen over night but if we work as a unit for the greater good of our people, plan productive goals and stick to them we can do anything.

Have you noticed that Street culture and rap music has breed a mentality where us as young people think we can get everything we want without working hard for it? Some elders call us the "microwave generation", meaning we tend rush things and expect satisfying results, which rarely happens. We need to first understand that there is no immediate rush, success will happen more quickly if we take our time studying and getting a full overstanding of whatever we want to do first, and not always think of the luxuries. Let's look at music for instance, it seems as though there is this big craze of our youth wanting to be M.Cs because of the illusion of the luxury lifestyle we see that comes with it. This clouds our vision of looking towards learning the business side of the industry, which is as important. Speaking of importance, it is important to know that not all of us are supposed to be M.Cs, many of us can help each other become successful musicians by playing the role of manager, A&R, stylist, promoter, music solicitor etc, which still makes you part of the music, you just make sure everything runs smoothly for the industry and performers which is just as valuable as being an M.C.

These are crucial elements that the music we love lacks. People like you and me that genuinely love the music, taking care of the music. Garage, Grime, and Hip Hop could be so much more successful, if we Overstood the importance of working as a team, where we can all play different roles to help the success of our music and still make good money.

There are so many different aspects of the music business in which we can use as a stepping stone to gain some experience first, before we become the star. A lot of people don't know that Sean Combs a.k.a P Diddy was a stylist for a male vocal group called Jodeci. He was even a backing dancer before becoming the owner of several multi million dollar companies. He gained a great deal of knowledge and experience before he became the person that we know today.

We need to start championing the importance of working together and running our own business's, also not just associating ourselves with sports and music. I'm not saying don't do sports and music, I'm saying we can do so much more. We have the potential to do anything in this world that we want to, SO LETS DO IT! Let's show the world what we are really capable of. And no, we're not doing it for them; we are doing it for us, for our people, so we can leave something great for the next generation to look up to and take further.

Knowledge is power!
When you apply it

Chapter Five

K nowledge is power! I guess everybody knows the saying it's probably been said to you a million times.

It has become very cliché, and I'd like to add that, we can have all the knowledge in the world, but if you don't use it then you are just another tree in the forest. It has no use just being in our head, knowledge becomes powerful when we apply it, then we will see the effect of its power.

It's kind of like a game (but it's a serious game), once we have gained a substantial amount of general knowledge we have to test it on people. Create conversations with other's you would class as having a higher intellect than yourself and see how the conversation flows, analyse how you articulate your words and speak on things that you have learnt to see if the person knows and understands what you are talking about, if they don't know teach them something, but don't be arrogant about it, if they do, learn from them so you can add to the information you already know. The brain is a powerful tool, use it to gain information and share it with others, that's how humanity progresses. Keep in mind you can never know everything, be a humble student and always research what others tell you so you know its fact. Even animals can teach you a thing or two.

We are living in what is called the age of information, there is nothing we cannot find out, the internet is a warehouse of knowledge, remember its here to help us.

We can definitely benefit from reading a whole load of books but we can profit even more through conversation with the highly educated. At first you may find it slightly intimidating but it's very useful. You'll learn words being used in different context, as well as learning new words. This will help you in knowing how to come across to different types of individuals, ultimately boosting your confidence. The more you do it the better you'll get at it. It's all about controlling words and knowing the art of when to use them. If you learn how to master the art of articulation, you can become very powerful and soon enough you will find it to be as natural as walking. If you're unsure about any words you hear people use in the outside world you don't know, the best thing to do is just ask them on the spot "what does that mean?" It doesn't mean you're stupid, it just means you're curious, inquisitive, diligent and willing to learn.

(If not when you get home pick up a dictionary)

"THINK BEFORE YOU ACT OR AT LEAST ACT LIKE YOUR THINKING"

You can generally tell when someone admires your intellect just by their face expressions and willingness to hold dialogue with you. Sometimes even when you ask someone what the words they are using means, they don't even know themselves.

Words are very important, because in today's society, they are the foundation of communication. If we take our time in studying words and their meanings we will have greater understanding of the language we use. We will be very clear spoken, easy to come across and easy to listen to, respectable people. That is if we can control our egos at the same time.

Having an abundance of general knowledge helps us move through life more comfortably and is very healthy for the brain, open your mind by getting out of your everyday environment, travel, go to museums, get acquainted with the world around you by studying other people, places and cultures, learn a Language. Our world is always changing and knowledge is the key to understanding it, pursue knowledge at all times but not to the point where you over feed the brain.

People can tell when you're a knowledgeable person. You have a confidence about you, you look more focused and your aura glows. You even start walking differently "shoulders straight head up" and if you dress as smart as you are then it compliments you emphatically. It's very important for us to take advantage of the world around us and be the best you can be. Do your best in memorising the truths you read in this book and try to apply it to your life, that's the only way we are going to see results. .Listen family What we have to realise is that the day and age that we are living in right now is very precious we should be so grateful that we are alive at this point in time this is the day that our ancestors were waiting for millions of years the time when access to all information was available for the world. Never in history has there been a time when so much information has been provided by nature. Nature is saying to us whatever we want we can accomplish and if we use our potential correctly we can change the world.

Don't believe you can, know you can

"DRESS AS THOUGH YOU WANT PEOPLE TO TRUST YOU"

Wasting time/controlling time

Chapter Six

I find that like myself, a lot of people have got a habit of wasting time. Time is one of the most precious things next to life; because once it's gone we can't get it back. In a world that's living, breathing and growing so fast, we need to grab every opportunity that we can. Every first, second, minute and hour of everyday, should be used to help develop and improve self and others.

We only have 24 hours in a day (which we sleep through more than over a quarter of) so we have to use the time that we are able to be active in, very carefully and be productive in it. If we're sitting down knowing that we're capable of doing something and are not doing it then you're wasting time.

If we're hanging around people that are doing nothing but wasting time, then we're wasting time! If we spend our day thinking more than we're doing, then again you're wasting time, unless you are thinking up a realistic plan.

What we need to start doing is controlling time; control when we are going to wake up and go to sleep, control what time we're going to eat our meals day to day, time when we're going to study, exercise, etc. This is called order and the opposite to order is chaos living in chaos is unproductive and one of human beings worst enemies.

Organise everything you do before you do it. It makes life so much easier to deal with and that is how we control time! If we want to better ourselves and access our 9 potential then we have to be disciplined and strict. The more we practise doing this, the more organised we will become as a person. The more we control our time is the more we will appreciate the free time we get. In time we will have the opportunity to appreciate the important things in our life on a day to day basis.

"THE HELPING HAND YOU ARE LOOKING FOR IS AT THE END OF YOUR OWN ARM"

Make a habit of getting yourself into a routine. Just like the police do routine checks, check that your routine is on point positive and progressive. Then nothing can stop us in achieving anything we want to achieve but ourselves.

Knowledge of self and kind

Chapter Seven

The word knowledge starts with the word know, so it is of great importance for us to know ourselves. I say know and not believe because we can believe in something 100%, and be 100% wrong. It's like walking with a blindfold over our eyes and hoping for the best. To know is to see clearly and seeking factual knowledge of self persons, places and the things around us will help us in understanding and overstanding life, thus it washes away confusion and makes the path to our destiny easier to see.

Having knowledge of self: as well as monitoring what our shoe size, cloth size and trainer size is (which should be a standard because as our body grow, it can sometimes change size without us noticing) we need to have knowledge of who we are. This includes knowledge of where we come from and an overstanding of where we are going to. Unfortunately a lot of us are not taking out the time to do so, which is one of the most important fundamentals of being the person you are and who you're supposed to become.

You might say: "What do I need to know my history for? It's not doing anything for me now".

But that's like saying "what does a tree need roots for? Or why does a house need a foundation, it's not doing anything".

The house you sleep in, if it did not have a strong foundation you wouldn't be bathing, going toilet, watching television, sitting or sleeping in it.

If some of the trees and plants never had roots, we wouldn't have oxygen to breath. We wouldn't have various fruits and vegetables to eat, plus some of the animals we eat wouldn't be able to survive or have the life for us to eat them.

So as we can see foundation is very important no matter which way we look at it.

NOW!
At school in our history lessons we learn about the Greeks the Romans, kings and queens of England (i.e.) Henry the eighth and his multiple wives, world wars, dinosaurs etc. We take in all this information that is very unimportant to Black (African) people, and then we leave school and do nothing with it.

(By the way, we get to watch Roots, which usually gets us angry and reminds us that we supposedly came from nothing)

If we took our time to study ourselves properly (where we really came from), we would hold very high standards, achieve greater things and know that it takes unity to succeed. We usually think that (our-story) not (his-story) starts at slavery.

NO!

It does not. Hundreds even thousands of years before slavery, we had great city's nations and society's, like Egypt, Nubia, Sumer, Cush, and Timbuktu to name a few. There are debates on whether the Sumerians were truly of Black origin amongst certain historians. I came across a book called "When We Ruled" by the author Robin Walker. On page 597 it states that the Sumerians called themselves the name "Sag Gigga" which actually means 'Black heads'. This would give an indication of what race these people were. It's a fact that the original people of this planet are Black; Africans/Nuwbuns/Ptahites.

We travelled to Spain as Moors in the 700's A.D and ruled for around 800 years. In this time we were building one of the greatest civilisation known anywhere in Europe. While this was happening, England was going through its dark ages, with streets full of dirt, mud, disease and barbarianism.

The Moors (Africans) brought fruits, built public streets, pavements, streetlights, drains and sewer systems. We wore silks, linen and also washed in the 900 (hundred) public bathhouses in "Cordova". Our ancestors, had thousands of properties, mansions and palaces with hundreds of schools and colleges.

So as you can see we were doing great things before the times of slavery. In what's known today as Egypt we constructed some of the greatest structures ever to be produced on the Earth's surface called Pyramids. To date no other people have been able to replicate these structures, and its secrets are still being held by Black (African/Nuwbun/Ptahite) people today.

We had our own culture and way of life back in "Egypt" also known as "Kemet" or "Tama-re".

As Olmecs we travelled over to what is now called South America and built there. We also were great sculptures, jewellers, mathematicians and masters in agriculture. Our ancestors had their own calendar and were responsible for planting the rubber trees in the South American region.

"THE ONLY TIME YOUR HEAD SHOULD BE HUNG DOWN IS WHEN YOU HAVE DROPPED SOMETHING"

Pyramids of Giza, Egypt/Tama-re

Again as you can see we were doing great things before the times of slavery. We are originators and creators, not followers and what you have just read is a small slice of our-story's cake which goes back millions of years.

If you look around the city that you live in today, most shapes of the buildings and structures are copied from ancient African architecture.

Things like building and inventing came so natural to us, but in recent times we hardly build and invent anything except music. Even if we are building and inventing anything of real substance, we usually don't hear about these Black (African/Nuwbun/Ptahite) individuals.

"WE ARE NOT THE CIVILISED WE ARE THE CIVILISERS"

From 1948 to the 50's, some of our Caribbean grandparents and great grand parents came over to England after World War 2. During that time we rebuilt this country with our bare hands along with the Irish. We rebuilt many buildings over the bombsites in the city. In some cases, our grandparents came home after working on the sites, only to find that we were kicked out of our homes for sometimes just missing one day's rent. Basically, we were not appreciated.

Not to forget that we also fought in the Second World War along side the British as well. As troops some of us even stayed here for a while, but after fighting the war. Once Hitler was defeated, the

British attitude changed towards us Caribbean's by saying things like "It's about time they went back home".

Around mid 1950's the British government needed Caribbean's to migrate to Britain. During the war, Britain had lost around half a million people, so the country had a big shortage of man and woman power. They needed us to boost back the economy and we were happy to come because we thought that England was the land of dreams. All in all over a period of time around a quarter of a million of us came over. After reaching England's shores we got nothing but overt racism, being called "darkies and niggers" and discriminated against.

But when we were needed to fight in the war, we were told that the motherland England needs you (funny how things change). We were treated with no respect, like many times before, but as we do we struggled and survived through it all by bringing colour, music, culture, good manners and cleanliness to this country.

We went from being turned away from hotel and houses, to buying some of the places we stayed in, through a self-constructed money saving system called Pardner. Groups of us would all work together on putting money into a kitty and each family would have their turn in receiving a sum of money each couple of weeks or months. While the local whites thought we were doing illegal activities like (drug dealing & prostitution) to get the money, we were just simply unifying in the given circumstances.

"WITHOUT OUR GRANDMOTHER AND GRANDFATHER, YOU WOULD NOT BE HERE

This was the 1960's and 70's, now just forty to fifty years later we know hardly nothing of these events, and the struggles our people went through. This should be common knowledge to us, as young Black males and females.

So if we can't respect the struggles we endured In England a mere few decades ago, how are we going to appreciate and respect what our ancestors went through during slavery 400 to 500 years ago? Respecting leaders like Paul Bogle, Marcus Garvey, Elijah Muhammad, Malcom X, Queen Nzinga and Nanny of the maroons etc.

Without our great people laying down the foundation for us from ancient Egypt right the way through to this very day today, we wouldn't have some of the freedom and great sense of worth that some of us have in this day and time.

"LIFE CAN ONLY BE OVERSTOOD BY THE PAST, BUT YOU MUST LIVE FOR THE FUTURE"

Now let's bring it right up to the families that we live in today. Do we even know the stories and struggles of our great grand mothers and fathers and their mums and dads and their mums and dads? Or do we still think our-story, foundation and genealogy doesn't matter. We have to start investigating and writing down our family's story.

We need to make sure our children don't forget them, because knowledge of them is knowledge of self. "This is something I myself have started doing recently, so I'm not acting like I am perfect or telling you what to do, I am just trying to help myself and my people".

Olmec head

South American Temple

Akhenaton

Haru, Asaru, Aset

The Sumerian Gods
known as the Anunnaqi

Goddess, Tiye

Goddess, Nefertiti

Coming off the boat

Empire Windrush

Elders reasoning

Family First

Chapter Eight

F amily first! I guess the title of the chapter speaks for itself. It is a principle that is of great importance, which some of us tend not to live by.

Our families are so close to us, and as much as we love them, they can get on our last nerve for whatever reason it might be.

We might hate them or dislike them, argue, fight and what ever else we do as families. Our Families sometimes do things to us that we wouldn't expect our enemies to do. And If they cross that line which you know they shouldn't have, then it is down to you whether you choose to forgive them.

But you know what "FAMILY IS FAMILY" and it's about knowing the nature of the individuals in our families, so that we can work around them. This is necessary in order to get the best out of the relationship with our families as much as possible, for the benefit of our families. Whether a particular family member is a thief, liar or jealous of us etc, we should try our best to talk through the problems we have with that family member. Always push it, one mile further to see if we can work it out.

As I said earlier "know the nature of your family". If they're a thief, don't leave anything of value around them or don't let them in our house or room, go to theirs. If they're liars don't believe what they say only what you see them do, if they're jealous they're jealous!

If you have a disagreement with a family member and there are children around, take the problem from around the children and sort it out rather than arguing, shouting and getting hysterical.

"YOU CAN'T CLAP WITH ONE HAND, WORK TOGETHER"

NOW!
On the bigger scale of things, the same principles apply. The problem with us Africans (yes Africans, because we are all apart of the African/Nubian/Nuwbun/ptahite family) today, is that we fail to overstand, an important principle that every other race in the world seems to live by except us: The principle of looking after our own first, and others thereafter.

WHY IS THAT?
What has made us so sick in the head, that we don't put Black people first for the benefit of our race? This is a topic that has run through every black household in the country (well I hope so). This is one of the reasons why some black businesses never seem to last long in our communities. One reason being, that we believe some of the stereotypical labels that are given to us, and, we simply don't see ourselves as family. It is very disappointing, because this is a problem that runs hundreds of years back into slavery. We have to

start valuing ourselves more and recognising the potential of us working as one family. Please Realise that, in reality, we are all the same people in the same situations trying to achieve the same results in varying degrees, but some of us do not respect the fact that, we can acquire all the successes in the world, but if our race family have not benefited socially and economically as a result of our successes, then it means nothing to our well being as a people. I won't be overly pessimistic, because there are Black people in our communities that recognise the law of "synergy" (look this word up) and are fighting to bring us back to the mental state of us living for and by each other, but to speed up this process, us as young people have to come to the realisation that if we don't work as brothers and sisters also, then our future will be disastrous. Did you know that Black people actually keep some Caucasian and Asian businesses afloat? Meaning that if we stopped supporting and buying from these shops they would have to close their business's down.

To me it looks funny seeing other races selling our products back to us (by that I mean it makes us look funny!). It seems we're like babies that can't look after ourselves. Instead of us keeping other businesses afloat, we need to start building and supporting our own. Therefore more money would be circulating around the Black community. This result would create more stability and togetherness among black owned businesses and naturally more employment for Black people as a whole.

There was once a documentary that came on T.V (*I can't remember the name or what channel*) when a black male T.V presenter, by the name of Darcus Howell was interviewing an Asian girl, and the young lady was categorising the different races within England, in a who is doing better than who kind of way. She described Black people as being at the bottom of the list. When I heard her say that, it really, really hurt me. The reason why it hurt me so much was because it was the TRUTH! WE ARE AT THE BOTTOM!

It wasn't the statement itself, it was that it came from another race, on T.V so the whole nation saw and heard it and I was embarrassed. We have been here longer than the Asian community and as a whole, it seems we are underachieving, that's just some of the reasons why we need to start putting family first.

There is a saying that goes: The Jewish community's money circles their community 10 times before it comes out of it, Caucasians 7 or 8 Asians 6 or 7, Black peoples money only circulates a disappointing 1 time. (Come on family we are better than this).

Discipline

Chapter Nine

D iscipline is one of the hardest things to carry out in the world today. This is because we are distracted or attracted by so many things that revolve around us, taking us off track of what we are supposed to be doing.

The world is moving so fast in recent times, information is at our fingertips (the internet) and everything is in our faces. That's why it's even harder to apply discipline that we can stick to, especially in our teenage years.

Let's look at Collins English dictionary's definition of the word.

Discipline: practise of imposing strict rules of behaviour,
    Attempted to improve the behaviour of
    (Oneself or another); by training or rules, able to
    behave and work in a controlled way

Without applying discipline in our life, we really won't get anything of importance done. It takes full control of the mind to practise discipline and maintenance of that control. The moment we start to loose control, the effects show straight away. On the other hand once we start practising it, it becomes easier to exercise and we'll be able to see that it's very beneficial to us.

Discipline is something that gets taught in the home first. Whether it comes from a mother, father or guardian, we all learned about what discipline was as children and it is an important principle that we should apply in all areas of life; from waking up in the morning at a specific time, to tidying up our rooms. Washing and ironing our own clothes (some of us don't do these things) down to little things like turning off our T.V and getting to bed at a certain time. It all takes some kind of discipline and structure to get these things done, which is something we will rely on as we grow from teenagers into adults.

If we haven't got the discipline to take care of the little responsibilities, then when the bigger things in life gets thrown our way in the future, we probably wont have it in us to take care of them either, and that's how we become a failure. So when our families are being hard on us about washing, cleaning and getting to bed at a reasonable time, you may not see it now, but you'll be grateful for being brought up with those disciplines in the future.

I've seen it so much in the Black community for some reason some of our youth/elders don't have the discipline to stick to something and see it through to the end, whether it is school, college, university or work. In some cases we can't be bothered, loose hope, pay more attention to having fun etc.

That's one of the many reasons why I felt that I had to write this book, we seem to be the people you don't want to be, and the irony is that everybody wants to be us (that's funny, but true).

When we do, do something in our right minds, nobody, yeah I said "NOBODY" does it better than us. We just don't give ourselves enough attention to really overstand the worth of our potential to even see a glimpse of what we are really capable of "do you get what I'm saying". IT'S CRAZY!

"THE KEY DOESN'T OPEN THE DOOR, YOU DO"

Some of it does actually boil down to us as a people having our own schools and education – "Another book; another subject".

Right now we need to deal with the way things are now!
We need to make life easier on our self.

These are just a few things that will help us to relax and be in the right frame of mind on a day to day basis:

Stretching

Nature walk

Twice a week workout

Deep breathing

Stretching:

Stretching is of up most importance to the human body. That's why so many people in the western world are taking up things like yoga and palates in modern times. It's very beneficial for us to practise the art of stretching at least once or twice a day if possible, with the application of deep breathing along side it.

It is something us as Africans used to do in ancient times, but have now forgotten. We called it "Smai" pronounced as "smie". If you bend down, and your finger tips cannot touch the floor without bending the knees, then that's a sign that you need to start NOW!

Refer to the book 'Afrikan Yoga' by Pablo M Imani.
ISBN: 978-1-906169-40-4

The reason why we need to breathe deep when stretching is because:

1. Its just simply the natural thing to do

2. It will help us to relax and focus when doing it

It's very meditative and it takes our mind off the pain, take your time when stretching there is no rush don't strain yourself.

Nature walk:

It's a fact that walking exercises more muscles than jogging or running does, so it benefits us to try and practise a relaxed walk at least once every two days for half an hour if possible.

It really depends on where we live, but most of us are surrounded by brick houses, blocks, main roads and road traffic. If we're surrounded by this everyday, believe it of not, it has a big effect on our brain and the way we look at things.

We need to keep our brain balanced, so we don't get too one dimensional. This can be done by something as simple as going for a nature walk. A nature walk is picking a local park where we live, that is mostly surrounded by natural life, trees, grass, bushes, flowers etc.

Just strolling and observing the beauties nature has to offer us, allows us to take our minds off the worldly things that can usually get us down. The best time of year to do this would be summer, because that's when nature comes to life. However don't let that stop you, because nature's beauty can be observed any time of year. It's very therapeutic and relaxing being away from the normal things we might do. It's about Giving time to ourselves; appreciating nature instead of spending our spare time in front of the T.V.

Workout:

A twice a week workout, the statement explains itself. A workout is a workout, it doesn't have to be twice a week, it can be three or four times a week, whatever works for us. However, don't go to the extreme, do what you can handle. A workout doesn't just mean working on our chest and arms; we also need to work on our whole body. This includes our legs, abdominals, shoulders etc, so that we can have a balanced exercise. Everything's about keeping an even balance!

We don't have to spend a lot of money going to the gym; we can simply start in our house or at the park.

Deep Breathing:

To breath deep is to use the full capacity of our lungs. Something which most of us don't do, so our bodies do not get the full benefit of the air we take in. Therefore the cells in our body are neglected of the normal oxygen levels that's needed for maintenance and survival.

If the cells are not getting what is needed to maintain themselves they start dying then our body is thrown out of balance which can be cancerous, so its very important to breath deep as much as possible. The only time we actually do breath properly is when walking and laying flat on our backs.

If we look at baby when lying on its back, we'll see the stomach going in and out, that's actually how we should be breathing. Our stomach should be going in and out the same way a baby's stomach would. When growing up, we begin to forget the practise of proper breathing.

Read this exercise then try it:

Put both of your hands flat on our stomach, around the belly button area.

Breathe in through your nose as deep as possible, so your stomach pushes both our hands out.

When you do it, hold our breath for 3 seconds and let it out through our mouth.

Try it now!

That's what we need to start doing to make sure we vitalise our bodies in the correct way.

Try that breathing exercise (breath in and out nine times) in the morning when you wake up, evening and at night before you go to sleep. It relaxes our body so we don't feel uptight and cramped. We can even do it when we feel frustrated or mad because it calms us down and helps us to think before we react.

Jesse Owens

The Greatest Black men on Earth

Chapter Ten

James Cleveland:

James Cleveland Owens was born in 1913 in a small town in Alabama. He came at a time that wasn't very prosperous for African Americans in the U.S because of the "Jim Crow" racism that was in effect at that point. His parent's were Henry and Emma Owens and their son was about eight years old when they decided to leave Alabama for a fresh start in Cleveland Ohio. On arriving Jesse was enrolled in a private school and on the first day in class the teacher asked him his name, rather than hearing J.C, she heard Jesse and from that point on he was known as Jesse. Jesse proved to be a hard worker taking on different jobs in his spare time delivering groceries, loading freight cars and working in a shoe repair shop. It was in this period of his life that Jesse realised that he enjoyed running and this relationship would be the spark that would help form one of the greatest black athletes the world has ever seen.

It was "Charley Riley" that spotted the raw talent in Jesse. During a gym class the students were timed in a sixty yard sprint and immediately he was invited to run in the track team. Jesse wasn't able to attend after school training due to his work responsibilities, so the coach offered him morning sessions. Being the talented quick learner that Jesse was, he quickly became a track star in Cleveland east technical high school. As a senior he tied the world record in the 100 yard (91 meter) sprint with a time of 9.4 seconds, only to tie it again in the interscholastic championship in Chicago. His name spread across many colleges and universities and many of them tried to recruit Jesse. He chose to attend Ohio state university at the age of around 19-20 where his competition on the track would be immense.

It was 1933 and Jesse would feel the direct effects of Apartheid. He was required to live off campus with other fellow African American athletes. When travelling with the team he would order carryout meals or eat at blacks only restaurants and sleep at black only hotels.

On occasions, "Whites only" hotels would allow black athletes to stay, but they had to use the back door when leaving as well as the stairs instead of the lift. On the 25th of May 1935, Jesse set three world records in just forty-five minutes. He was able to achieve this despite the fact that he had back problems leading up to the event (he fell down flights of stairs and had to receive treatment up until the race).

Jesse was convinced he could still participate. After convincing the coach he ran the one hundred yard (ninety one meter) sprint, where he tied for the world record again. Each timer clocked him in at an official 9.4 seconds and he went on to participate in the other events.

Just a mere fifteen minutes later, he took his first attempt at the long jump, and shattered the world record (which was twenty six feet, two and a half inches, not bad for an athlete with back problems). Despite the pain, Jesse soldiered on setting a new world two hundred and twenty yards (two hundred and one meters) sprint record in the time of 20.3 seconds. The next event would be two hundred and twenty yards hurdle, which he completed in 222.6 seconds, another world record. Jesse accomplished a task that had never been done in the history of track and field.

By the end of the year at Ohio State, Jesse had then realised he could compete at a more competitive level. He entered the 1936 Olympics, which at the time was known as the "Hitler Olympics" in Nazi Germany. Adolf Hitler was going to prove to the world, that the German Aryans where the dominant race, however Jesse had different plans in mind.

Jesse won gold medals in the one hundred meter; two hundred meter, long jump and the four hundred meter relay team rendering him the first American in the history of track and field to win four gold medals in a single Olympics. In all but one of these events Jesse again beat world records but this time it was all Olympic records. Jesse's impact on the Germans was so great that they named a street after him, after he had died. Despite Jesse's success he was not offered endorsement deals because he was black.

Other than being a great athlete Jesse was very articulate and became a public speaker. He travelled around the country speaking for companies such as Ford and the United States Olympic committee, in 1976 Jesse was awarded the highest honour a civilian could receive, the Medal of Freedom. Jesse prevailed in the face of racism and segregation with his natural talent being the greatest African athlete in sport of his time. He died March 31st in 1980 at the age of 66 from cancer.

Johnnie Cochran

Johnnie Cochran:

Johnnie Cochran Jr. was born 1937 in Shreveport Louisiana. He was the great grandson of a slave. As a child Johnnie was groomed to have academic excellence, racial tolerance and independence. When Johnnie was around six years old his family moved to Los Angeles California where the young man saw things that opened his eyes and inspired him to achieve great things in life.

He came across friends that had great wealth being that he integrated well. He attended public schools where he earned very excellent grades. He was known to have great debating skills and earned a reputation for it being that he liked arguing. He went on to earn a bachelors degree in business administration in 1959 and proceeded to get a (J.D) degree from the Jesuit Loyola law school in 1962. By 1963 Johnnie took a job as deputy city attorney in the criminal division where he worked as a prosecutor.

In 1965 he entered private practise with a criminal lawyer by the name of Gerald Lenoir after which he started his own firm called "Cochran Atkins and Evans". Later he encountered his first taste of fame, when he represented a widow (who wanted to sue several police officers after they shot and killed her husband), while he was trying to rush her to the hospital, she was pregnant at the time. This was one of the first few cases that Cochran ended up losing alongside another memorable case in the early seventies where he would work in the defence of a former Black Panther by the name of Geronimo Pratt. Pratt was accused of murder, and although

Cochran lost the case, he pressed on for a retrial, sincerely believing that Pratt was framed by the police.

It seemed Cochran leaned towards defending cases against people of colour, as well as individuals who suffered police brutality. He went on to establish a name for himself within the Black community.

Although Cochran found great satisfaction in being a defence lawyer, it wasn't doing much for his image. In order to refashion himself and gain political strength, he became a lawyer at the Los Angeles county district attorneys office. Although it was a good career move, it didn't stop the racist police from harassing the great black man that he was.

One afternoon he was driving across town with his two daughters in his Rolls Royce when he was pulled over and told to get out of his car, with his hands up while the police had their guns drawn.

They searched through Cochran's possessions and suddenly they realised who he was after coming across his 'number three badge' from the D.A office. Both officers where apologetic and after that incident, Cochran never got stopped again. Mr. Cochran never did publicise the incident. After spending five years of working at the county's district attorneys office, Cochran went back to private practise in 1983. Reinventing himself as the "best in the west" he opened Johnnie L. Cochran JR law firm. One of his first major victories would be in the case of Ron Settles. A college football player who corrupt police officers stated that he had hanged himself in a cell after being picked up for speeding (come on now!).

Cochran demanded that the athlete's body be examined. A coroner determined that he had been strangled by he police choke hold. A pre-trial settlement got the grieving family seven hundred and sixty thousand dollars. This wasn't the first time Cochran went up against the police and it wouldn't be the last, it is estimated that he has won up to forty three million dollars for his various clients in his career.

As Mr. Cochran's fame grew, more celebrities began to gravitate towards the great lawyer. From pop star Michael Jackson (who was accused of child molestation, in which the case was eventually settled out of court) to Todd Bridges, (the different strokes star who was accused of attempted murder, in which Cochran got the case acquitted). There were many more celebrities that favoured Cochran, such as Tupac, Snoop Dogg and P.Diddy.

One of his well publicised cases would be the Rodney King where three white and one Hispanic police officer was accused of assaulting a Blackman (Rodney king) by hitting him with their batons up to fifty six times. Their argument was that he was speeding and tried to resist arrest when they stopped him. The incident had a big effect on the Black community and it resulted in them rampaging through the streets of L.A in what's known as the "L.A riots". It went to trial and the officers were eventually acquitted because the mostly all white jury couldn't come to a decision. However, the most publicised case of his career would be that of O.J Simpson. Simpson was accused of the murder of his ex wife Nichole Brown and her friend Ron Goldman. Simpson was an ex American football player turned T.V star. The charge shocked the white American public the most, being that Simpson was black and his ex wife was white.

This case had coverage all over the world and was filmed for the whole of America to follow step by step. Cochran was part of Simpson's defence team, which he eventually became the leader of. Cochran being the analytical and diligent observer that he was, presented a very strong case for the ex American football player. He addressed the many holes in the prosecutions case against Simpson and highlighted the racist attitude of Mark Fuhrman, one of the investigating officers.

One of the components that would be apart of the prosecutions strong points was a 'black glove' that supposedly was used in the murder of these individuals. The glove didn't actually fit the big handed football player, so one of Cochran's quotes that would stand out was "if the glove doesn't fit then you got to acquit".

Cochrane being the controversial and up right lawyer that he was, displayed brilliant and sincere arguments throughout. In summing up the case, he said that Simpson had been set up or framed by a racist police officer. Cochrane argued that if such an injustice were to be ignored and allowed to persist, it could lead to genocide as practised by Nazi Adolf Hitler. Many people would describe Cochran's remarks as "the race card" but Cochran wasn't apologetic about where he stood on the matter. After a long trial

Simpson was awarded a not guilty verdict. This was another great victory for Cochran and the Black people of America. Cochran would become known as the most famous lawyer in the world and went on to represent more African Americans. He even wrote a biographical book, and opened a firm that practised civil law. All in all Cochran just wanted to make race issues disappear within America. He most definitely played his part in working towards that goal, in the field that he was in.

He was a great human being that accomplished a lot in his line of work and became wealthy doing the honest work that he done.

Mr. Cochran died at his home in Los Angeles on Tuesday 29th of March 2005 from a brain tumour.

Influential Black Women

Oprah Winfrey, Rosa Parks, Lauryn Hill
Angie Stone, Winnei Mandella, Iyanla Vanzant

The Great Marcus Garvey

"Be proud of our race today as our forefathers were in the days of old, we have a beautiful history and we shall create another in the future that will astonish the world. I can advise no better step towards racial salvation, than organisation among us. We have been harassed trampled upon and made little of, because of our unfortunate condition of disorganisation"

"Always think yourself a perfect being and be satisfied with yourself"

Marcus Garvey:

Marcus Garvey was born in the West Indies (Jamaica) on August 17th 1887. Garvey is said to be a descendant of the Maroons through his father. The Maroons were African slaves who forced the British to recognise their independence.

As a young man Garvey was analytical and very diligent like his father. He was well educated in a range of subjects from History to General Knowledge, as well as many others. He worked as an apprentice to his godfather, who was a printer, who kept a library that Garvey used frequently.

Garvey eventually became the youngest printer in Kingston, at the young age of 18 (which was a big achievement after moving there). As time past Garvey became very concerned with issue's that surrounded his people. He saw that Black people were not treated as equals to other races. He felt that he could help make a change and started to practice public speaking. Garvey took elocution lessons from a black politician named D.R J Robert Love as well as studying the speaking styles of many church ministers.

The young aspiring public speaker eventually went on to publish his own newspaper called "Garvey's Watchman" around 1910.

Garvey eventually left Jamaica in 1910 at the age of 23 and travelled through central and South America. He visited places such as Costa Rica, Panama and Guatemala, making a presence everywhere he stopped off. Garvey also travelled to England in

1912, where there were small pockets of Africans, Jamaicans and other people of colour. He found himself in places like Parliament, Birbeck College and Speakers Corner. He went on to visit places like France, Italy, Spain, Austria, Hungry and Germany. As we can see, this was a brother that was on a mission. Garvey found himself back in London by 1913 and found a job for the newspaper called the "Africa Times". While he was there, he met an Egyptian born man named Duse Mohammed Ali, who was also an actor and had a big influence on Garvey's back to Africa mission. Garvey left England in 1914 and continued his travels. Everywhere he went from America across Europe to England, he always had the interest of African people at heart.

Sincerely wanting to make a change, his experiences would be the moulder that shaped him in becoming one of the greatest leaders, and well known Africans in our and his-story.

After leaving England, Garvey went back to Jamaica. At the age of 27 he founded the U.N.I.A (Universal Negro improvement association). The U.N.I.A spread from Jamaica to South Africa, Nigeria, Cuba, Trinidad and Tobago, Guyana, Dominican Republic, Barbados, Virgin Islands, Belize, Panama, Costa Rica and there were many other places where U.N.I.A branches would reside. It is evident that this movement had gained influence all over the world. The U.N.I.A also had its own newspaper called "The Negro World".

Garvey's main mission was to get Africans back to Africa. One of his well known slogans was "Africa for Africans" words that echo in the minds of Africans all over the world. Garvey wanted to get Africans back to Africa by way of travelling by ships. A shipping company called the "Black Star Line" was a business venture that Garvey would pursue, in the hopes that Africans would be able to trade all over the world. This mission however, was stopped by the Bureau of Investigation, later to be known as the Federal Bureau of Investigation (F.B.I). The F.B.I began to collect information on Garvey and built a profile on him as being a radical, for the purpose of deporting him back to the West Indies. The investigation was headed by a man named J. Edgar Hoover. Garvey was also heavily criticised by W.E.B Dubois and Rev. Robert W. Bagnall, two African Americans that would influence the deportation of the great leader.

There was even an assassination attempt on Garvey's life, by a former employee named George Tyler. His secretary at the time, Amy Ashwood, risked her life by grappling with Tyler, and forcing him to flee. Ashwood would later on become Garvey's wife.

Marcus was eventually sent to prison for mail fraud. The prosecution claimed that Marcus knowingly mislead shareholders into thinking they would make some kind of profit, using an empty envelope as evidence against him. Garvey did have a lawyer at first, but would later go on to represent himself, saying that his lawyer made a deal with the judge. He spent over 2 years in prison and was then deported back to Jamaica.

Garvey saw the lack of our own spirituality, self-pride, economic independence and unity amongst Africans all over the world. He refused to sit around knowing that something needed to be done and not do it. Garvey had an inner urge to mend the dysfunctions that he saw amongst us, and acted upon it. He is a true warrior that we can all learn something from and he should never be forgotten. Garvey is to be remembered just like the quote "one god one aim one destiny". We should all take our time to study the life and work of Marcus Mosiah Garvey, using it as a guide line, so that we can utilise his successes and learn from his mistakes. Otherwise we are basically saying that his mission was in vain, which would be a big disrespect to all of our ancestors. Garvey eventually died in the United Kingdom on June 10th 1940, after suffering from Asthma, Pneumonia, and Strokes, he was just 53.

Tupac Shakur

Tupac Shakur:

Tupac or Makaveli was born June the 16th 1971. Born Tupac Amaru Shakur, his mother was Afeni Shakur, a member of the Black Panther movement, which still exist today. Prior to Tupac's birth, his mother and twenty other Black Panther members were arrested on charges of an alleged conspiracy to blow up several buildings in New York. Being the strong woman she is, she represented herself in the case that eventually got thrown out.

She spent sometime in the woman's house of detention of Greenwich Village whilst pregnant with Tupac in 1971. She was released and came out with hopes to raise her new born child in the rough area of the Bronx and Harlem. As time went on they found themselves having to sleep in homeless shelters. She, Tupac and his sister travelled around frequently seeking better surroundings to live in.

By the age of 12 whilst living in Harlem Tupac's mother enrolled him in Harlem's 127th street Ensemble where he got his first acting debut as "Trans" in the play "A Raising Sun" Tupac would later recall it as "the best shit in the world". By 1984, the family moved to Baltimore, where Tupac finished high school. Having transferred to Baltimore School of Arts, where he studied poetry, jazz, acting and dance. It was here that Tupac wrote his first rap and also won all the rap competitions he had entered in, being considered the best in the school.

Tupac was known as a bright, funny and easy to get along with person during his school years. It was here, where he met one of his best friends "Jada Pinkett" a friendship that would last until his death.

It wasn't long before Tupac's family was on the move again, this time to northern California, to a place called Marin city. It was here that Tupac began indulging in illegal street activity such as selling drugs and other things of that nature. Tupac moved out of his mother's house and moved in with Leila Stienberg (a Caucasian woman) with his friend Ray Luv at the age of 17. She was like a literary mentor for Tupac. He read several books there and it was noted that his intelligence was well ahead of the average student his age. By 1989 Leila helped organise a concert for Tupac's group called "Strictly Dope" at the time.

The successful concert, lead him to meet up with Atron Gregory, who set him up with "Digital Underground", a Hip Hop group he auditioned for in 1990.

Digital Underground was from the Bay area in northern California, Tupac was hired as a backing dancer for the "Sex Packets" album tour of the U.S and Japan. In early 1991 Tupac featured on the group's single "Same Song" from the album "Sons of the P". He also appeared in the movie "Nothing But Trouble" where in it he played himself in the same year of 1991.

By 1992 Tupac had put together his solo album "2pacalypse Now" where he said his album was aimed towards young black males. He also starred in a film called "Juice" that same year, which showed the public, that as well as rapping he had great acting skills. Both talents lead to more movies and more albums.

Another album "STRICTLY 4 MY N.I.G.G.A.Z" went gold in just a few months having two popular and memorable singles "I Get Around" and "Keep Ya Head Up". The film "Poetic Justice" also came out that same year where Tupac shared the big screen with pop star Janet Jackson. Although Tupac's talents were doing great for him in climbing the ladder to success, trouble seemed to follow this young black brother wherever he went.

He was accused of sexually abusing a woman in 1993, in an incident that happened in the hotel he was staying at. He had always denied the charge, however the incident still went to court. On the 30th November 1994, a day before the verdict was to be announced, Tupac was shot 5 times in the lobby of Quad Recording studios in Manhattan.

He blamed rapper Christopher "Notorious B.I.G" Smalls, and music producer Sean "P Diddy" Combes for the incident, saying they set him up. Despite his injuries Tupac appeared in court the next day. On December 1st 1994, he was found guilty of sexual abuse charges. He began his sentence on Feb 14th 1995, and shortly into his sentence he released "Me Against The World". This multi platinum selling album, would make him the first ever artist to have a number 1 album on the billboard charts, while serving a prison sentence.

By 1995 Tupac's case got an appeal, but due to his legal fees he couldn't raise the 1.4 million bail money needed. However after serving 11 months of his 1 to 4 year sentence, the C.E.O of Death Row records, Marion "Suge" Knight, posted the 1.4 million dollar bail money. This was in exchange for Tupac being obligated to release three albums for the Death Row music label.

Tupac had already written a large amount of material, so immediately after leaving prison he went straight into the studio and started recording. He also formed a rap group called "Outlaws" and recorded a diss record called "Hit Em Up". This track was aimed at Notorious B.I.G and Bad Boy records. The U.S media used this to magnify an East coast verses West coast feud, and in doing so blew the whole situation out of proportion.

Tupac went on to release his next album since being released from jail called "All Eyes On Me" (which sold 9 million copies) and after that another album called "Makeveli". Throughout his career, Tupac made an impact on people from celebrities to the poorest of poor people on the streets, being that his music reflected the reality of the streets and the world around us.

He was a rebel, leader, talented, smart, poetic but some what confused individual that maybe went so far into the deep end, that by the time he was trying to pull himself out, it was too late. After a Mike Tyson boxing match on September 7th 1996 Tupac was involved in a fight with a man named Orlando Anderson. The Death row entourage attacked Anderson in the lobby of a hotel, which was caught on Close Circuit Television.

After this incident Tupac got into Suge Knights car and went on his way to a club owned by Death Row at the time, called club 662. Before he actually got to his destination, a car pulled up next to his side of the vehicle and discharged a firearm.

Tupac was shot twice in the chest, one in the left arm and one in the thigh; he died 6 days later in hospital on the 13th of September 1996.

All of these Black men were great in what they did in the time that they lived in. They stood out because of the work in which they had done and the divine talent behind it. I am not saying that they were perfect, (because no one on this earth is, and yes some were greater than others, but that goes without saying). However there are different degrees of greatness. It all depends upon what we are doing, and the perception of the onlooker. These individuals were some of the greatest Black men on earth in their time, hence the title of this chapter.

What I would like to add is that all of these great brothers are deceased and have gone back to the essence. This chapter that you are reading right now is entirely dedicated to you holding this book in our hands. I wrote a summary about the lives of these brothers to show you that they are just like you. You probably realised that all these brothers (except Marcus Garvey) are American. Does it really matter where they are from? They are African just like you. They started off with drive, ambition and made something great out of it. The result of which has in graved their names in his-story and our-story. The same ability is within you right now. What I'm trying to say is the greatest Blackman and woman on earth is YOU, yes YOU holding this book in our hands.

"EVERYTHING IS CREATED FOR SOME USE, HOW ABOUT YOU"

You have to tap into that greatness (9 potential), which we all have and nurture it. Help it grow and know that you are on this planet, on a physical journey for a purpose. You need to find that purpose, fulfil it and be very serious about it. If you can read what these brothers have been through and achieved, and not know that you are great then you are offending our own self. You are them and they are you, so whether its music, politics, sports, law or building an empire, be great in that which you do because you are the greatest man and woman on earth. "Spot the difference book 2" we will cover the greatest females on the planet earth, the Black female.

Other Influential Black men

Dr Martin Luther King

"There is nothing more tragic in this world than to know right and not do it. I cannot stand in the midst of all these glaring evils and not take a stand".

"The tragedy of physical slavery was that it led to the paralysis of mental slavery"

The Honourable Min. Louis Farrakhan

"When you feed the human mind garbage, you destroy the beauty of the mind and lessen the power of the mind to perceive reality"

The Great Malcolm X

"When you live in a poor neighbourhood your living in a area where you have to have poor schools, when you have poor schools you have poor teachers, when you have poor teachers you get a poor education, poor education you can only work on a poor paying job and that poor paying job enables you to live again in a poor neighbourhood, so it's a vicious cycle"

Where are we now?

Chapter Eleven

Well if I go by the context that's in this book, we are not in our right minds. Our vocabulary is weak, we don't structure our lives properly, we are wasting time, and we don't know our's-story as opposed to his's-story. By not putting our African family first, this shows that we are not setting a good example for the youngsters that are coming up, as well as those that are yet to be born (there's a lot we have to clean up).

I often hear elders or even adults my age (which is 25 at the moment) say "what has happened to our youth" or "we didn't used to act like that when we were their age". There is some truth to that, yes some of us were as rebellious as some of the youth that are walking the streets today. However the difference is that we had more respect for our elders and the value of life was more precious than it is today. The value of life is still dropping rapidly, and one of the main reasons is that we are influenced by the lifestyle of rappers from the U.S as well as movie characters.

If we do want things to change we have got to be real with each other about these facts. We hear what some of these rappers are saying on their records, and we actually start believing some of the crap they are talking. In fact it's worse than that, because we are trying to emulate a surreal lifestyle (I have been guilty of emulating the lifestyle of rappers too). We look up to these Americans, and this is one of the reasons why we are influenced in wanting to live like them, which is not going to work in the U.K.

Some of us use Hip Hop as a way of escaping our own reality, and the repetitiveness of this result's in us living in this escape world. Yes the lifestyle does relate to us insofar as we go through similar things, but then we start taking on other attributes of that lifestyle which is detrimental to us.

It's a fantasy that some of us are chasing which results in us wanting everything now (microwave generation), disrespecting our females, quick to kill another brother and loosing touch with self. All from rappers over exaggerating their lives, and in most cases this is done in order to entertain the masses. Exploiting the whole gangster image because sex, violence and drugs sells. These rappers get supported by major record labels that don't care about the negative effects the music has on young minds, they'll continue to fund these artists as long as they make a profit. This breeds the mentality of, if I act like a gangster my records will sell, which over shadows the positive and conscious rappers like Common, Nas, Mos Def, Talib kweli and many others. Even when we hear rappers beefing with each other some of us actually think it's real. LOOK!

The music industry has turned Hip Hop into a sport, like wrestling. It is all to build hype, which encourages sales. People therefore accept it as real, which is what they want. It drags us into the beef and we are then drawn into buying the next mixtape or album, in order to hear what else they are going to say or do. Once we have bought it, then they have done their job. They have influenced us to spend our money. They become the voices in our heads, shaping our lives and lifestyles daily. When we listen to something religiously it's bound to have a big influence on us, whether we like it or not.

It seems our youth can't go through a day without listening to music, mostly Hip Hop, and when we analyse it, most of the things that we are hearing are not positive. Almost every other line is "my bitch" "my gun" "Shoot this nigga" "smoke this weed" "I'm getting high" "get drunk" etc. This all breeds death and destruction.

Now look at what is going on around us and tell me if it doesn't reflect those things what you just read. It's sad but true!

I myself have been slowly maturing and moving away from this way of thinking and lifestyle, because I have seen it for what it is. Destructive! It does nothing for the improvement of our race. Hip hop needs to be brought back to its essence, and its up to us to do it.

Yes there are positive things within Hip Hop like Black people that run million dollar companies such as clothing lines, trainer lines, drink companies, rappers that have opened homes for the homeless as well as community centres etc.

"SHORT STEPS ARE SAFER THAN BIG LEAPS"

Unfortunately, we don't seem to be focusing on that, because it is blanketed by so much of the negative aspects of Hip Hop. We look at the surface rather than scratching past it and studying what is behind the music videos, DVD's and CD's. The young black mind is attracted to this because it looks fun and easy to do. We are looking at people having fun in videos and think that is all there is to it, when that is not the case. As I said earlier in the first chapter, we have to be very careful what we tempt our mind with because it's one of the hardest things to control. Once the personal attribute called the ego gets hold of it whether good or bad, after being repeatedly fed it becomes a wild animal that is hard to tame, and that is what some of us are acting like now, wild animals.

As well as T.V and music another tool that captures our young minds is computer games that emulate this animal nature of gang wars, drug dealing, swearing etc. Now, these "adult games" are being played by children. It plays a very big part on how they view life and how they think the world is. These games are filled with black faces, negative music, and are actually teaching our youth how to become sophisticated killers. Even on camera phones, the youth can get hold of pornographic and violent images; they send it around to each other, which to them is fun. However, the question has to be asked "what is it doing to their state of mind?" They are becoming lower natured instead of tapping into that higher Godly self, 9 potential. Now this is a general summary on some of the negative things that are taking place within the Black community, which I am not going to make over shadow some of the positive things that are happening around us that some of us don't hear of.

"THE BEST EXERCISE FOR OUR BODY IS TO WORK OUR MIND"

School:

In 2006 GCSEs Black pupils gained the most improved results of any ethnic group according to figures released by the government. It's important to know that when these figures are being monitored they categorise Africans and Caribbean's separately. The portion of Black Caribbean pupils achieving five good GCSE results at grades A* to C or the equivalent qualifications was up by six percentage points to 41.7% with 48.3% of Black African pupils achieving the same.

So basically we have improved our GCSE results compared to other ethnic groups, but we are not leading. Chinese and Indian pupils are the ones that are leading currently which I think has a lot to do with how they are raised at home, and the mindset they are groomed to have as well as a concentrated effort their parents apply on achieving. Another thing to note is that girls consistently perform better than boys in GCSEs. This applies in all ethnic groups, so boys we need to start catching up. As far as exclusions, Black Caribbean's were the most likely to be excluded as well as other blacks and mixed white according to 2003/4 reports. The over all positive that we can see, is that since 1998 Black African GCSE results have consistently climbed in percentage as well as Black Caribbean since 2003. This should be a natural thing anyway, because we are supposed to exceed that which is before us, so let's make sure that we continue to do so.

Raising your game to reach your full potential

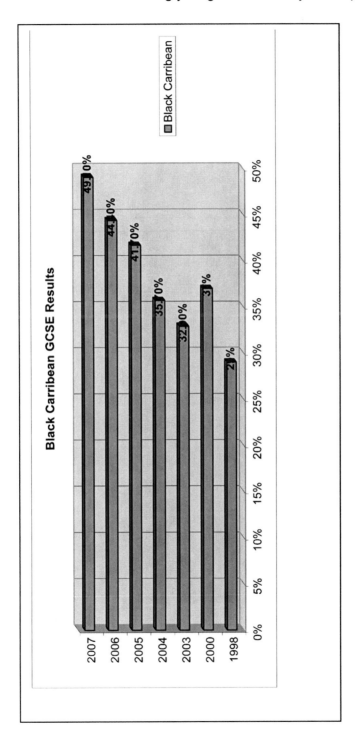

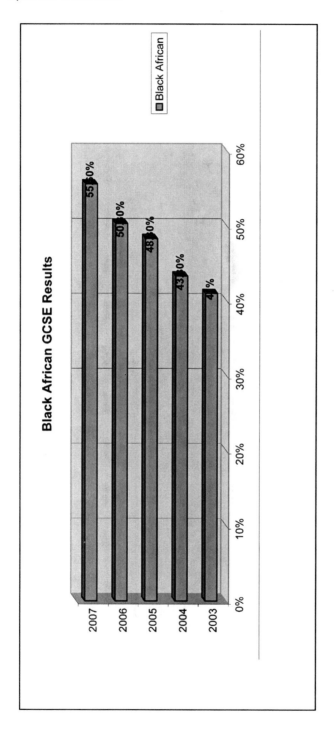

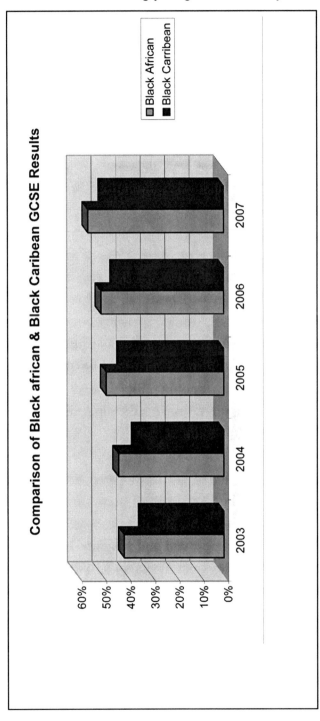

Black Business:

According to statistics, so called ethnic minorities are more entrepreneurial than whites. Also, in recent years black owned businesses provide jobs for over 70,000 people and had a total turn over of almost 4.5 billion and growing. Black Businesses also make up 4% of the business population in London with over 10,000 organisations.

Black women are running at least 25% of businesses. The few biggest industries for black owned firms are real estate, wholesale and retail trade. Black owned business tend to be smaller than the average business leaning more towards sole proprietorship or partnership, rendering 61% of black owned businesses having 1 to 4 employees, this seem to have an effect on the support from the community being that people don't tend to support small businesses because they feel more safe with big companies and its just not a common thing to do so.

We also have this disease of not supporting ourselves. There was a time when black businesses would predominately flood certain areas (such as Brixton, Tottenham and Harlesden), and this, if continued, would have improved and sustained our economy. Since we are not supporting our own businesses, today, as our elders did, we have lost our presence significantly within the British economy.

We still play an important role in the economy, in so far as we have become more of a consumer for businesses run by other races, as opposed to producing and providing products and services, for our selves and others.

This has a knock on effect, such that more blacks are ending up in prison than university. We are not being encouraged to become entrepreneurial, as a result of lack of business presence in our community. (We have a lot of work to do).

Black men in prison:

Statistics have shown that since 1997 the number of African Caribbean's being imprisoned had leapt 58% and 90% of prison inmates are black. Basically since the Labour party went into power it has raised dramatically.

(I wonder why). The fact remains that we can't always look outside ourselves for blame; the problem is within us, although judges do tend to give more custodial sentences to Black people than others, and heavy ones at that.

The report called "race equality in prisons" found that for every 100,000 white people in Britain, 188 were in jail. But for Black people the figure was 1,704 which meant that Black people are 9 times more likely than whites to end up in prison, which shows that race has an important effect on how decisions are made.

In order not to mislead you, just over a third of Black people in prison actually are from overseas making up around 5.63 percent of the U.K prison population. The black British make up 8.9 of all prisoners in the U.K according to recent studies. The U.K has the highest prison population in Western Europe and the Black African family has made a significant contribution to those figures.

We need to start changing this around, because the age of the youth going to prison is getting younger and younger, especially with the gun and knife crime situation. We are acting like devils just killing each other with no care what so ever and there is no particular reason for this it's a conglomeration of reasons. Another thing that I find with the youth of today is that some girls are loosing there femininity. Acting like boys in the way they talk and dress i.e., tracksuits, hoods, jeans hanging off there behinds, boisterous mannerism's and walking on the street with their hair all over the place plus smoking a lot of weed. All of this makes them come across very dopey and old in the face before their time. Boys also are looking older before their time talking and looking dopey as well as wearing tracksuits and hoods regularly, not looking after their appearance, plus a concentration on street activities more than their future.

However it's not about the problem, it's all about the solution, which is another reason why I felt I had to write this book. I probably would of wrote a song about my feelings on this subject a few months ago but I've found that its going to take a lot more than a song or album to fix this problem we have in our communities, or even a book for that matter, but its another step in my contribution to help. It's an image and example of what someone like my self could do other than street activities, becoming the solution rather than the problem.

Remember, the power of God is in our hands, use them to uplift and unite rather than to degrade and bring destruction.

Where are we now? Like I said at the bottom of society, the only way is up, if not we will carry on regressing and perish as a people.

Taking Action

Chapter Twelve

"*TODAY IS THE LAST DAY OF YOUR LIFE, IF YOU DON'T DO ANYTHING WITH IT*"

The easiest thing to do right now, would be to read what is in the contents of this book, be inspired by it and not act on the inspiration it has given you, forget about it and carry on with what you was previously doing before you picked the book up. That would be very easy!

That would mean that you do not care about yourselves your friends ancestors our immediate and Black African (Nuwbun/Ptahite) family, which would be a very sad thing.

This book was inspired by the Creator and our ancestors, speaking through me to give to you. Do you know how I know that, because there were times when I was writing certain parts not knowing how powerful the words I was putting together were until I went back over it. I'd say to myself: "how did I write that, why did I write that and what made me put it in that way"? The information was just coming straight through me, and I wasn't going to neglect it, I knew I was tapping into my higher self and I loved the feeling of it.

I was laying down in my living room and I got the feeling that there was something I needed to share with my people. It was a feeling that made me feel excited and scared at the same time. I was excited because of the challenge and scared because of the responsibility. I knew it was going to be a task and a big leap insofar as the commitment and change that I had been going through for a long time. I now had to be ready to face the challenge and go forth with it publicly. It has been an inner battle and I knew that this book would be the symbol of that change. This is because I would be sharing things with you like you was my own immediate family, and talking from a leader kind of perspective. Not that I want to be a leader, its that I have no choice but to be a leader, seeing what is going on with my people, I can't just sit back and watch, acting like everything's okay, when it is not. It's like my ancestors were saying, "you're qualified to do this but it's your choice if you want to do something about it or not".

I have always been committed to my people one way or another but now it's really time to be a man about it 4REAL!

I thought who better but me, I'm known through my music, people know my face and even look up to me, its no coincidence, everything happens for a reason. I just have to show, prove and try to help do things right, for the betterment of my people. It didn't just happen like abracadabra (poof) and I started writing (NO). Like I said I was lying down on my sofa, scared more than excited and I needed a second opinion. So I called a sister and friend of mine by the name of Femi and we talked. Then in the middle of the conversation I nervously said "I want to write a book you know" and she was like "ok so why don't you do it". It was like I was expecting her to say something negative like "do you think you can handle that" or something like that. Not that Femi is a negative person, it's that I was the one that was negative or pessimistic, and that's what was actually stopping me from "TAKING ACTION". I was being extremely pessimistic, but when she so eloquently but nonchalantly said "so why don't you do it" it all made sense. I was like for real I'm going to just do it AND I DID!

"IF YOU'RE NOT GOING TO GET ANYTHING DONE TODAY, GO BACK TO BED"

As soon as I got off of the phone with her I got my pen and pad and started writing down the chapters and the title came to me straight away "spot the difference" when I saw it in front of me I said yep, "this is it" and I haven't looked back.

I said to myself it's going to be for the youth, it's going to be straight to the point easy to understand but I'm going to use words that they're going to have to pick up the dictionary a few times to get the meaning of. I'm not going to talk down to them neither, I'm going to talk about the problem and give solutions and if the youth are seriously going to follow what is in it and apply it to themselves, people will be able to spot the difference in them. So here we are the last chapter!

Hopefully from reading the previous chapters you are now ready to take action, (ITS ALL ABOUT YOU RIGHT NOW). I have tried my best to equip you with everything you need to start your journey of self improvement and development (NOW ITS DOWN TO YOU IF YOU WILL ACT UPON IT OR NOT). You would be silly not to, if you are not on the journey to better yourself at the moment, now is the time to start. If you have gotten to this last chapter, then you are already on the journey anyway. So take your time step by step and don't look back always think and be positive about things and put yourself around like minded people, whenever you feel like you are going off track, let this chapter or any other chapter in this book remind you about what you are supposed to be doing and get back on course. If you think it can help a friend read it to them, borrow it to them or tell them to buy it. I hope the information has helped you in every way possible and that the creator and ancestors continue to guide you in all that you do, from myself, your brother, and friend, thank you very much for reading my first book "Spot The Difference".

Objective concentration:

Objective concentration is to place our full attention on an object without breaking that concentration for as long as possible. It's very beneficial in helping us being able to focus on what ever we need to do and calm our brain from over thinking when it's not necessary.

The best object to use through my experience is something like a fruit. Make sure you're relaxed and in a room which is comfortable, with no disturbances. We should switch off any thing that can distract us, such as the television, radio mobile phones etc. You can sit on a seat or on the floor with our legs crossed if that's comfortable for you. Our legs don't have to be crossed though! Place the object at least two and a half to three arm lengths away from you and you are ready to start, take 9 deep breaths just to prepare yourself.

People often make the mistake of thinking when we concentrate on an object, you're meant to just concentrate on just looking at this object and that's it. This is not necessarily true if you are a beginner, what you want to do is concentrate on it but think of everything you can do associated with that object. So if you're concentrating on something like water, you look at the water and you start to associate the water with other things you can use it for. You can drink water, bath, shower, water a plant, boil, swim, it rains water our body is 70% water etc. anything associated with water you can aim your focus towards is good for your concentration. The moment you loose focus or think of anything that is not associated with water (like something you done earlier that day) you start again. The more we practise the longer we will be able to hold our focus, time yourself if possible so you know you are improving.

At first you may think "this is long" but trust me you will see and feel the benefits if you put time and effort into it. These are the things we need to do to get our minds focused once again in order to tap into that 9 potential.

If you can successfully do this for a 10 to 15 minute period of time, the next step is to place our full attention on just the object without thinking about what else you can do with it.

If this seems to hard there are other forms of concentration exercises we can utilize to develop greater concentration.

Such as:

1. Doing the alphabet backwards Z Y X W V U T....... I'm not going to write all of it, work it out for ourselves.

2. Counting from 100 to 1 down in three's.

For example: 100 97 94 91 88   85............And so on!
Close you eyes when you do this it helps to enhance your concentration. If you make a mistake its important that you start again and try harder, this develops a "I wont loose mentality" when you count down from 100 you should end up

finishing like this (10   7   4   1) when you get to the number 1 work our way back up like this
(1   4   7   10) All the way back up to 100.

We should be able to count from 100 down to 1 and back to 100 again without making any mistakes practise this at least once a day before you go to bed, if you master it continue to practise it and do it with your family and friends, the benefits are incredible.

We will have more advanced exercises in "spot the difference book 2"

I find this exercise very beneficial myself, there is a secret formula to it, it isn't actually that hard once you do it a few times, it becomes impressed upon your sub-conscious mind.

Appendix

All sayings in this book are taken from Dr Malachi Z York (aka Baba).

His-Story
The definition of his-story is everything the Caucasian/white man has documented from his perspective about the world and other races that are in it.

Our Story
The definition of our-story is the things that we as Black/Nuwbun/Ptahites have written about, and for us, from our perspective.

Overstanding
The definition of overstanding is to know the full mechanics and result/outcome of a particular person place or thing; the when where, why, what and how.